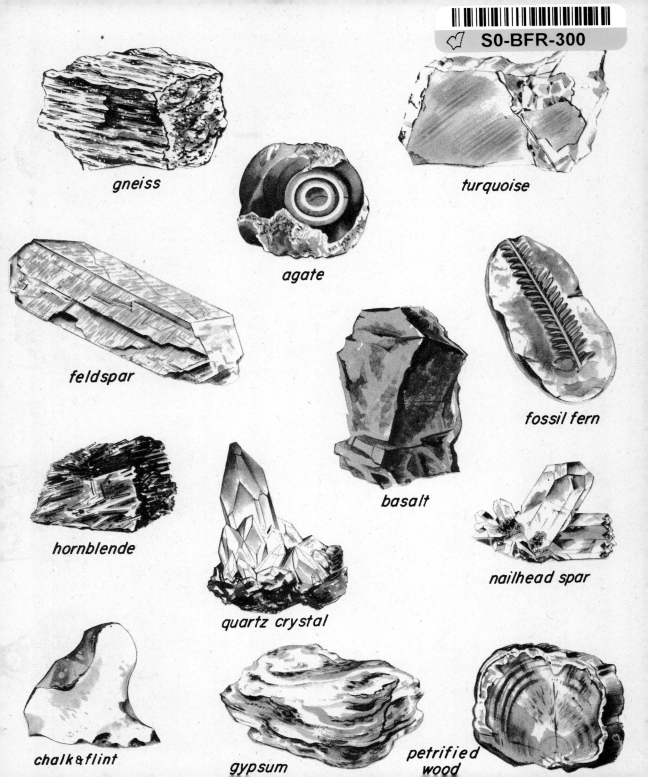

gneiss

turquoise

agate

feldspar

fossil fern

basalt

hornblende

quartz crystal

nailhead spar

chalk & flint

gypsum

petrified wood

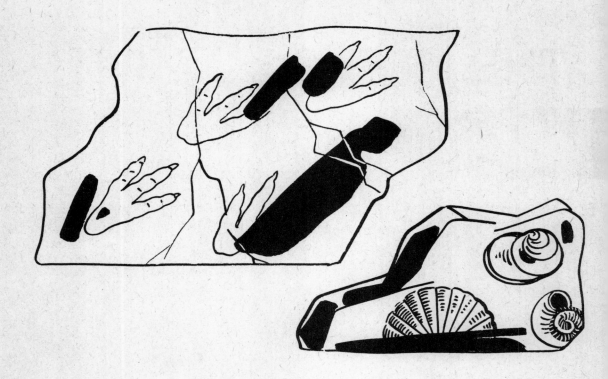

The author's thanks to Percy E. Raymond, Professor of Paleontology, Emeritus, Harvard University, and to editor Mary Elting.
The artist's thanks to David Jensen, Head of the Department of Minerals, Ward's Museum, Rochester, N. Y. and Richard Hughes of the Rochester Museum of Arts and Sciences, for all their advice and help.

Eleventh Printing

Printed in the United States of America by Polygraphic Co. of America, Inc.
Published in Canada by Ambassador Books, Ltd., Toronto 1, Ontario

THE FIRST BOOK OF

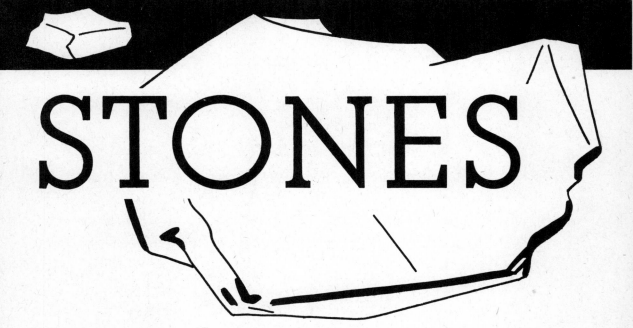

STONES

By M. B. CORMACK
Director, Roger Williams Park Museum,
Providence, Rhode Island
Pictures by M. K. SCOTT

FRANKLIN WATTS, INC. 699 Madison Avenue, New York 21, N. Y.

YOU WANT TO BE A COLLECTOR

Perhaps you don't know one stone from another—very few people do. But perhaps you have collected some stones already, because they were pretty or odd-looking. You'd like to know what they are, where they came from, and what they are made of. This book answers your questions.

When you make a real stone collection, you have to be a detective. You have to hunt for clues that will answer the questions: What is it? What is it made of? How was it made?

You can't always tell, just by looking at a stone, what it is. But you can make tests that will give you clues.

YOUR DETECTIVE KIT

Every stone detective needs these things to work with:

A knife or a steel file for scratching the stones

A piece of glass to make scratches on—get a piece

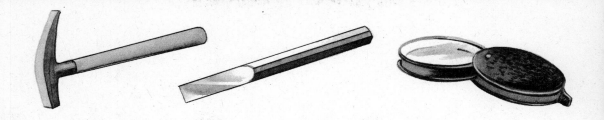

with smooth edges so that you won't cut your fingers.

A magnifying glass for examining the stones closely

An ordinary copper penny

A piece of white tile—the kind that is used on bathroom walls or the kind that is put under hot dishes on the table

A small bottle of plain fizzy soda water—(or ginger ale or any soda pop will do)

You will also need these tools:

A *hammer* for breaking your rocks open. Very often the outside of a rock has been stained or colored from lying around in the earth. You can tell what it's like inside only by breaking it open. Many hammers are not strong enough to break stones, so collectors try to use a special hammer that has a flat end for breaking stones and a sharp one like a chisel for splitting them.

A *chisel* for chipping small pieces of stone from bigger ones. This should be a rock chisel and not a wood chisel from your tool chest. Wood chisels will be spoiled if you use them on stones.

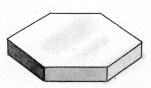

YOUR FIRST TEST

Now you are ready to make your first test.

Look over your stones and see if you have one that has a dull shine and is almost pure milky white. It may be a large, polished-looking pebble from a beach or from the edge of a stream. Or it may come from a graveled road or even from a graveled parking lot in town.

Break the stone with your hammer -- you will have to hit it quite hard. See if it is all milky white inside.

Hold a piece of it up to the light. Can you see through the thin edges? Then perhaps your stone is *milky quartz.*

Next, take the penny, the knife and the piece of glass from your testing kit. Rub a rough edge of the stone over the penny. The stone should scratch the penny.

Try to scratch the stone with the knife. Quartz is very hard, and steel can't scratch it.

smoky quartz crystal

quartz crystal

milky quartz crystal

Now take the piece of glass and rub the stone across it. Press down about as hard as you do when you are rubbing out marks with an eraser. Does the stone scratch the glass? If it does, you almost certainly have quartz. The only stones harder than quartz are valuable stones and gems — diamonds, rubies, emeralds and some others—and you probably won't find any of these lying about in the road to pick up.

Quartz is called a stone, but it has another name, too. It is a *mineral*. Later on you'll find out more about minerals.

Quartz is not always milky white. It comes in almost every color. This is because little bits of other minerals are mixed in with it. The minerals that color quartz act like dyes. No matter how you dye cloth, it is still cloth. So, quartz of any color is still the mineral, quartz.

Usually you find quartz in rough chunks called *massive quartz*, but quite often you can find *quartz crystals*. They often occur in little pockets in other rocks. Quartz crystals have six smooth flat sides. They come to a neat point on top. Once in a while you may even find a double-ender! The sides always meet at the same angle, no matter what size the crystal is. Some quartz crystals are very tiny and there are giant ones almost as large as you are.

On page 31 you will find out what makes crystals and why all quartz doesn't come in crystal form.

Each special kind and color of quartz has its own special name. You will be surprised to find how many common stones are varieties of quartz.

There is *agate*—real agate, not the imitation kind you find in toy marbles.

There is *amethyst*, which often comes in beautiful large crystals. Its usual color is deep purple but around the iron mines of Lake Superior it is often a deep blood red.

There is *flint*. Indians used it to make their arrowheads.

There are *opals* and *onyx* and *carnelian* and *jasper* —all used in jewelry.

But no matter what its color, each of these specimens is quartz, and each one is hard enough to scratch glass.

flint arrowhead

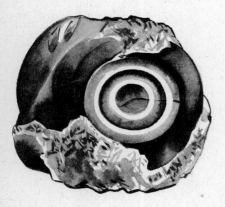

agate

YOUR COLLECTION IS STARTED

Now you have tracked down your first stone.

Next you should number and label it. A good collector does this the moment he finds out what it is. On the label he writes the number, the name of the stone, and the place where it was found.

Cut out a small square of adhesive tape. On it in dark ink write the number 1, and stick the adhesive on the stone. Then make a neat paper or cardboard label with the information you have about your specimen:

1 Milky Quartz Pebble Pirates Hill Conn.

Set the stone on the label, place it on a shelf or in a box, and your collection is begun.

On page 77 you will find the best ways to keep your collection so that you can work with it and show it to your friends. You will find ideas for making the work easy and lots of fun.

YOUR SECOND TEST

Suppose you break a piece of white glossy rock that seems very hard. It will scratch a penny. A knife won't scratch it. But, when you rub it over the piece of glass in your kit, the stone will *not* scratch the glass!

You thought you had a piece of quartz, but the test proves you haven't. Quartz will always scratch glass easily.

Now try bearing down a lot harder as you rub the stone on the glass. Press about as hard as you do when you try to cut a very tough piece of beefsteak with a dull knife. Now can you make a little scratch?

If you can, you probably have a stone called *feldspar*. Its name means "field stone."

Feldspar will also scratch the flat blade of your knife.

It won't be long before you can tell feldspar from a chunk of quartz just at a glance. They do not shine in the same way. Feldspar shines like a polished china plate. Quartz shines more like glass.

12

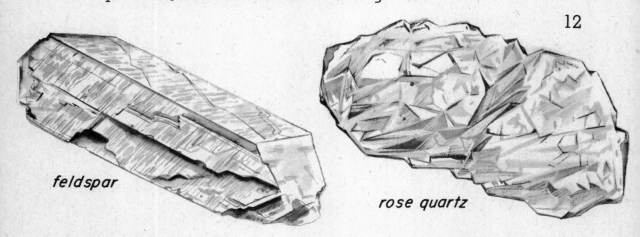

feldspar

rose quartz

Meantime you can make another test. Take a hammer and strike a spare piece of feldspar. It breaks clean in two directions and almost clean in a third. It breaks into little slanting bricks, like matchboxes that have been blown a little bit askew by the wind. The angles at the corners aren't quite right angles. The sides of the bricks lean.

But quartz never breaks clean in any direction. Take a hammer and try it. The breaks are jagged and rough, with no good, flat surfaces.

When a stone breaks clean, with one or more flat surfaces, we say it has cleavage. Feldspar breaks easily.

Feldspar may be pink or white or even bright green. Beautiful green feldspar called *Amazon stone* comes from Pikes Peak, Colorado. White and pink feldspar are common almost everywhere. The colors are caused by bits of other minerals that have dyed the feldspar.

Make a label and you have the second specimen for your collection:

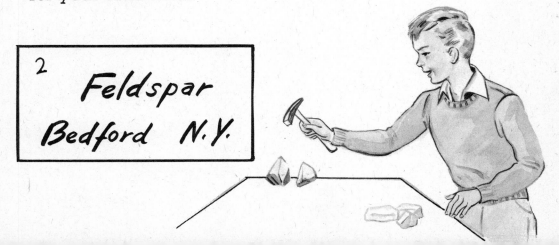

2
*Feldspar
Bedford N.Y.*

YOU CAN EASILY FIND THESE

Feldspar and quartz are the two kinds of mineral you will be most likely to find all over the world. Indeed, they are the most important minerals in the world. We could not live without them. They form the largest part of granite rocks, that are the very backbone of the earth. Clay comes from feldspar, and much of the earth's good farm land is clay soil.

White beach sand is mostly quartz and feldspar. The tiny grains are bits of larger stones that have been chipped off and ground fine as the stones knocked and rubbed against each other, perhaps for years.

When feldspar grains are crushed to powder, they make fine clay. Probably your dishes at home are made of feldspar clay. Bricks are made of it, too and are colored by other powdered stones to reds and yellows.

YOUR THIRD TEST

The easiest place to find your next specimen is right in your own house. Take apart an old-fashioned electric light fuse. The little window in the fuse, which may look to you like plastic, is really a thin piece of mineral. It is called *mica*.

14

glass making

You will be most likely to find good-sized pieces of mica if you live in North Carolina, Virginia, the Black Hills of South Dakota, New Hampshire, northern New Mexico, the eastern slopes of the Rocky Mountains in Colorado, or the country around Franklin, New Jersey. But you can find small pieces, mixed with other things, in stones all over the United States.

You can always tell mica by the way it splits into thin, perfectly flat layers like paper. Scientists call this *cleavage in one direction.*

MICA
Creede, Colorado

Mica is flexible—you can bend it.

Mica is elastic—it can snap back.

Mica is transparent—you can see through it.

Mica is shiny—it shines not quite like glass or quite like a pearl. We call the shine of a mineral its *luster*.

Mica is soft—you can scratch it with your finger nail, or very easily with a copper penny.

Mica is fireproof—it will not burn. That's why it's so good for artificial snow on Christmas trees. Mica is also used to make snow storms in filming movies.

White mica is called *muscovite* because it was once much used in Muscovy, the ancient name for Russia. There, sheets of it were made into window panes.

Black mica is called *biotite*. It has been stained with iron. Mica may also be brown, yellow, pink, gray or greenish.

A STONE THAT FIZZES

Perhaps you have broken open a piece of white stone that doesn't seem very hard, not nearly so hard as quartz or feldspar.

There is an interesting test for this one. Put a piece of quartz, one of feldspar, and a spare piece of your new specimen each into separate small dishes. Now open a bottle of vinegar and pour a little over each one of the specimens.

You will find that the quartz and feldspar will not do anything. But look at your new specimen. See how it bubbles up!

The fizzing shows that your specimen belongs to a group of rocks that contain a substance called *lime*. But you can't tell exactly which kind of lime rock your specimen is until you make another test.

feldspar

limestone

Try to scratch the stone with your copper penny. Press down very firmly. If the penny does not leave a mark, try scratching the stone with your knife. If the knife leaves a scratch, your stone may be *limestone*. (You can read more about limestone on page 43.) Or your stone may be marble (see page 57).

If the penny, pressed down firmly, does scratch the stone, and if the stone scratches the penny, then both are of the same hardness, and your specimen is probably a mineral called *calcite*.

Calcite may remind you of feldspar, but it is much softer. It is also much more transparent, or easier to see through. It has a different shine, and often you can see rainbow colors in it as you turn it this way and that.

Limestone is a mixture of calcite and other minerals. A few kinds of limestone contain so much calcite that they are soft enough to be scratched by a penny. So you must make one more test to be sure that your specimen is really calcite.

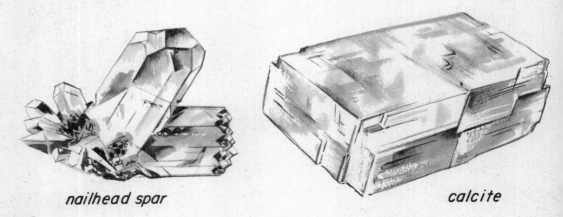

nailhead spar   *calcite*

This test is for cleavage—are there any clean, flat surfaces when you break it? Remember how you split the piece of feldspar? It broke clean in two directions and quite well in a third. Calcite breaks in three directions, so that three flat surfaces come together. It also breaks into slanting bricks, but these won't fool you. Feldspar will scratch calcite, but calcite can't scratch back!

Limestone sometimes flakes off into flat layers but this is not true cleavage.

So, your stone is calcite and you can make that label for it if it passes these tests:

1. Did it fizz when you poured soda water on it? Yes.
2. Was it just as hard as a penny? Yes.
3. Did it break clean three ways? Yes.

We haven't asked its color. Usually calcite is white but it may be stained pink, yellow, green, blue or brown.

Next to quartz and feldspar, calcite is the commonest mineral. It forms part of many sorts of rocks.

19

You will be sure to find calcite if you live near caves where there are stalactites and stalagmites. These look like stone icicles hanging from the ceiling or sticking up from the floors of caves. This is how they are made:

Water, seeping underground, passes over limestone, which has calcite in it. Tiny amounts of the calcite dissolve in the water, just as sugar does in tea. In limestone country, the action of water eats out caves in the rocks. More water seeps through the ceilings of the caves. As it drips, some of the calcite sticks to the roofs or dribbles to the floors. So, mineral icicles are formed, and the drip builds upside-down ones on the floors below. Often these icicles grow together and form weird fairy halls full of pillars in strange, fantastic, and often beautiful shapes. Sometimes they are even stained red or brown by iron. There are many such caves — the Mammoth in Kentucky, the Luray Caverns in Virginia, and many famous ones in Bermuda. They are very common in the limestone country of the South. Tom Sawyer and Becky Thatcher lost themselves in a limestone cave.

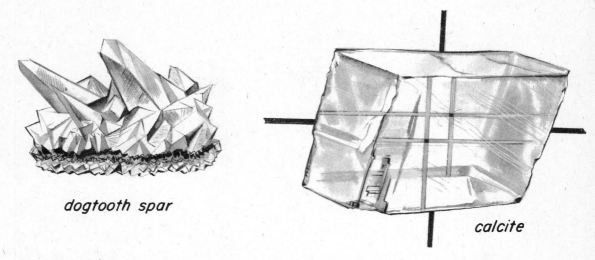

dogtooth spar

calcite

Sometimes calcite comes in crystals. The picture shows you some of their shapes.

SEEING DOUBLE

Some time you may see a valuable calcite specimen of a very different kind. This is clear calcite — so clear that you can actually see through it, but not as you see through a piece of glass. When you look through this amazing piece of calcite you see everything double! Its name is *Iceland spar* and it is very valuable for use in microscopes.

But it is still calcite and you can make exactly the same tests for Iceland spar that you made for any of the plain white or colored varieties.

If you want to own a piece of clear calcite, you can buy it for very little money. Any science museum will give the name and address of a mineral supply house.

Hornblende

A HARD ONE TO FIND

All the stones you have in your collection so far are minerals (unless that limy piece was hard enough to be limestone).

There is one other mineral, called *hornblende*, which you should know about. You may not find a piece of it all by itself, but you might find some bits of it in the granite rocks you will read about on page 27.

Hornblende is a dark mineral, black, brown or dark green. It is quite hard. You can barely scratch it with your knife. It comes in long, slender crystals. It is opaque — you can't see through it.

THE HARDNESS SCALE

Your tests have proved that some stones are harder than others. Real collectors have a regular way of grading stones. This is called the *hardness scale*. All minerals fit into the hardness scale somewhere. They may be from hardness 1 up to hardness 10, which is the hardness of diamond.

Here is the scale:
Hardness 1.

The softest stones belong here. You can scratch them easily with your finger nail. A pearly white stone, talc, has hardness 1. Talc is so soft it is used to make talcum powder. Any stone as soft as talc has hardness 1.

Hardness 2.
You can scratch stones of this hardness with your finger nail but not so easily as you did talc. Gypsum and some mica are hardness 2. All No. 2 stones will scratch the No. 1's.

Hardness 3.
Here you use your copper penny. Your finger nail won't scratch stones of this hardness, but the penny will, if you press down hard. Calcite has hardness 3, and so do some kinds of mica.

Hardness 4.

Now you have to use your knife. A penny will not scratch stones of this hardness, but the knife will scratch them easily. You will find stones in this group later on.

Hardness 5.

You can just barely scratch stones of this hardness with a knife. Hornblende has this hardness.

Hardness 6.

A knife won't scratch stones in this group, but the stones will scratch the flat blade of the knife. They will also scratch glass if you press down quite heavily. Feldspar has hardness 6.

Hardness 7.

Stones of this hardness will scratch glass. Quartz has hardness 7.

Stones of hardness 6 and 7 — feldspar and quartz, for example — will scratch stones of hardness 1, 2, 3, 4 and 5. That is an experiment you can try.

Scientists carry their hardness scale up to 10. Topaz is hardness 8. Corundum is hardness 9. You might find a rough piece of topaz, but it isn't common. Precious topaz is a gem stone. Rough topaz and rough corundum can be bought for very little money from a dealer. Precious corundum is called ruby if it is red and sapphire if it is colorless to deep blue. Rubies are often more valuable than diamonds, especially pigeon-blood rubies of a deep red color.

Diamond is hardness 10. It is the hardest stone in the world.

As your collection grows, you will probably read other books about stones, and you will find that when a new stone is mentioned, its hardness is usually given by number. You can always go back to this hardness scale and find out how to test a new stone.

ABOUT PUDDINGS

Now your collection has four minerals in it — quartz, feldspar, mica and calcite. You know about a fifth mineral—hornblende. You have found all of them except the fifth in separate chunks. But most stones are not as simple as these. Most stones are mixtures.

You know that we mix all sorts of separate things together in cooking. These things we call ingredients.

Most stones are made up of many different ingredients. Stones made of a mixture of minerals should be called rocks. Hot liquid rock has a name that means *dough*. One rock is called *pudding stone*. You can even see the things in it. Many rocks were really cooked deep down in the earth.

Your five minerals are very important rock-ingredients. They have been mixed or squeezed or cooked with each other or with other minerals to make many kinds of rock. By using some of the clues you have already discovered for these minerals, you can track down new stones that are mixtures. If you wonder how such hard ingredients ever got mixed together, you will find the story about them on page 30.

granite

GRANITE

One of the mixtures you are most likely to find is *granite.*

A piece of granite is fairly hard to break open — not so hard as quartz or feldspar, but you may have to give it several good whacks with your hammer.

The inside is usually gray and speckled-looking. With your naked eye you can see that it is made up of coarse grains or small lumps of light and dark minerals. Use your magnifying glass to examine them for cleavage planes.

The glassy ingredients of granite are quartz.

The white or pink ones with a dull shine to them are feldspar. Always look for the clean breaks of the cleavage planes in the feldspar when you break open a piece of granite.

In granite, the papery-thin flecks that you can separate with your finger nail are sure to be mica.

The solid black flecks are likely to be hornblende.

Other minerals do occur in granite, but these are the four common ones.

27

GRANITE

Granite may come in many colors and shades. The most common kinds are gray and pink granite. The feldspar determines the color of the granite, but impurities in the feldspar may turn it yellow, green or even brownish red. You may be sure that the red color came from iron.

You can often find granite in mountains or hilly country where clumps of rock stick out through the soil, and it can be found everywhere if you can just dig deep enough. The map shows the main places where granite crops out above the surface of the earth. Notice how much granite is on the eastern coast.

Granite is very strong, so it is used to build bridges and buildings. A curious thing is that granite buildings aren't indestructible. If the wooden parts of a building burn, they heat the rock. The tiny particles of water that are imprisoned in the quartz are turned to steam. The steam expands and cracks and crumbles the rock, so that it is useless for rebuilding.

Granite is a good stone to work with because it chips nicely into blocks. Also it can be polished until it shines and, once it is polished, no water can seep inside to crack it.

Even if you live far from any granite hills you can easily get a specimen of this rock. Just keep your eyes open for buildings of gray stone or visit a stonecutter's yard or a monument-maker's shop. There will surely be scraps of granite for you to pick up.

Most of the granite you see in building stones and monuments is fine-grained. Coarse granite is called *pegmatite*. You can hack out great chunks of its mineral parts. If the chunks of each mineral measure a foot across you may call it *giant granite*.

granite quarry

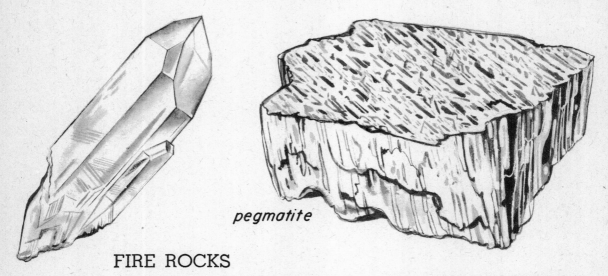

pegmatite

FIRE ROCKS

How did quartz, feldspar, mica and hornblende ever get mixed up together to form a rock in the first place?

This is a question every stone collector asks.

The answer is very simple. They were *cooked* together before they got hard.

Scientists have a name for a cooked stone like granite. They call it an *igneous* or *fire* rock. Igneous comes from the Latin word for fire.

There are as many kinds of fire rock as there are ingredients to make it.

Long ago, igneous rock was not hard solid rock at all. It was hot and liquid, and all the minerals in it were mixed up together. Slowly it cooled and hardened, but in some places it stayed hot longer than in others.

It made a great difference how slowly the hot liquid cooled. This is why:

30

As the liquid cooled, tiny crystals of the various minerals began to form. Gradually the crystals grew bigger. Crystals really do grow — but not exactly as living things do. They grow in an orderly way, and they need time and space to grow in.

The longer it took for hot liquid rock to cool, the larger the crystals in it became. Giant granite cooled the slowest of all.

Each mineral has its own true crystal shape, just as birds and flowers have their natural shapes. Quartz crystals have six smooth flat sides. Mica comes in flat six-sided crystals. But often mineral crystals are so crowded that they do not get room to grow properly. This is what makes massive quartz — the kind you find so commonly.

THERE ARE ROCKS STILL COOKING

Hot liquid rock is called *magma*. Magma in Greek means dough. You can knead bread dough with your hands, but rock dough must be pressed and squeezed by tons of rock, often miles below the surface of the earth.

rock dough

If the dough was granite dough, the rock became granite. If the dough was made of other minerals, it made a quite different rock. (You don't get blueberry muffins or chocolate cake from bread dough.)

There is magma today, hot and liquid, far below the surface of the earth. It is squeezing along toward the surface to form new rocks just as it has done since the beginning of things. Nobody knows quite how it pushes its way upward. The liquid rock fills in cracks, forces its way between flat layers of other rocks. It pushes up the rocks over it and folds them into mountain ranges. Sometimes it finds a weak spot and flows out peacefully to cool on the surface of the earth.

All this takes a long, long time. You can't see mountains growing except in a few odd places of the earth where volcanoes suddenly pop out of the sea. In the long chain of the Aleutian Islands that reach out from Alaska toward Asia, this has happened while men were watching it!

cross section of earth's surface

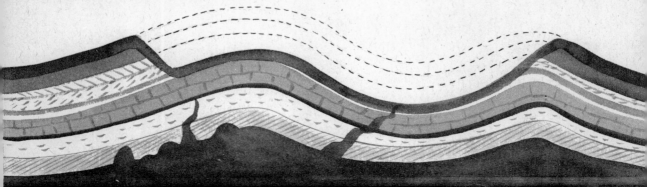

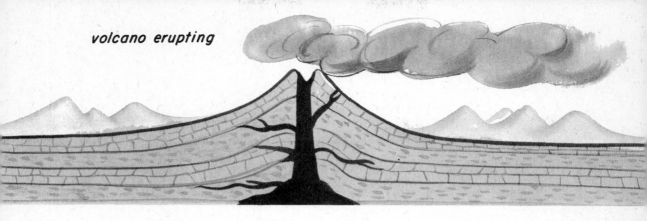

volcano erupting

Often the magma shakes the rock layers and we call it an earthquake. Or the magma blows out violently through a hole in the earth and we say a volcano has erupted or gone off.

ABOUT VOLCANOES AND LAVA

The magma that spills out of a volcano is called *lava*. Lava often cools so fast that it doesn't have a grainy look like granite. The ingredients stay mixed smoothly together and don't separate into little grains or lumps.

Scientists think that many volcanoes were made like this:

The hot magma flowed upward till it struck rocks that had water in them. The fiery magma turned this water into steam. A little steam will lift the lid of a tea-kettle or drive a steam engine. A great deal of steam has even more force. It can blow a hole right through the crust of the earth wherever it finds a weak spot. So steam and lava were flung high into the air. Much of

33

obsidian

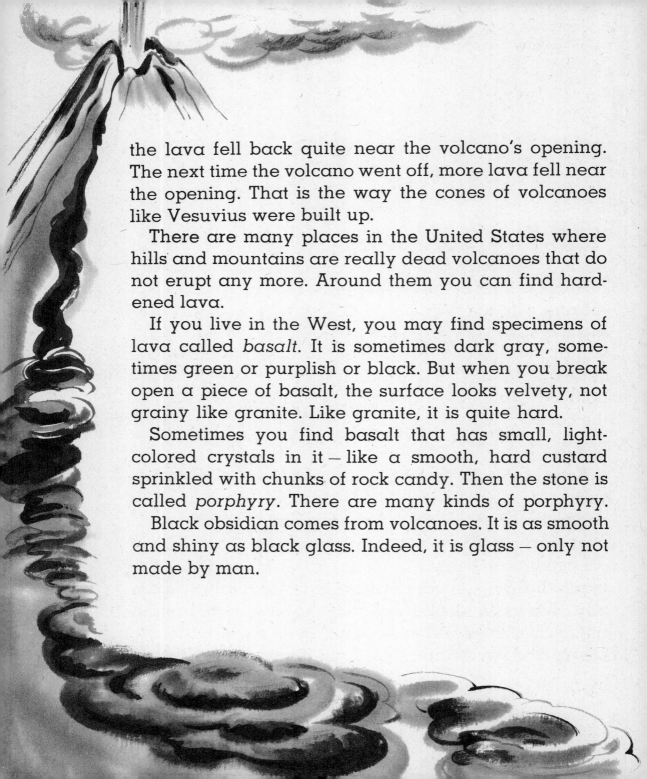

the lava fell back quite near the volcano's opening. The next time the volcano went off, more lava fell near the opening. That is the way the cones of volcanoes like Vesuvius were built up.

There are many places in the United States where hills and mountains are really dead volcanoes that do not erupt any more. Around them you can find hardened lava.

If you live in the West, you may find specimens of lava called *basalt*. It is sometimes dark gray, sometimes green or purplish or black. But when you break open a piece of basalt, the surface looks velvety, not grainy like granite. Like granite, it is quite hard.

Sometimes you find basalt that has small, light-colored crystals in it — like a smooth, hard custard sprinkled with chunks of rock candy. Then the stone is called *porphyry*. There are many kinds of porphyry.

Black obsidian comes from volcanoes. It is as smooth and shiny as black glass. Indeed, it is glass — only not made by man.

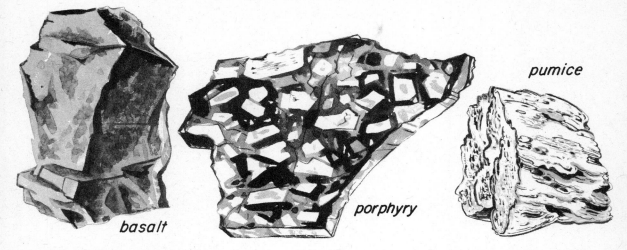

basalt

porphyry

pumice

Another kind of lava is called *pumice*. It is spongy-looking and so light that you can lift easily a large block of it. It will even float on water. The curious thing is that pumice has almost the same ingredients as a heavy piece of basalt. It is really the hardened foam of boiling basalt — just as meringue on lemon pie is really the cooked foam of egg white.

ROCKS THAT COME IN LAYERS

As soon as the first fire rocks hardened, millions of years ago, something began to happen to them. They began to wear out, and they have been wearing out ever since!

First, water attacked them. Rain poured down on mountains and washed away any loose chunks or particles on top. Rivers carried the stones along, bumping and knocking them together until even pebbles of hard quartz were ground into sand.

35

Rain seeped down through cracks in the rocks and froze into ice. The ice split the rocks apart so that more chunks could be carried away by floods. Glaciers crept down mountains, pushing and rubbing and banging stones together, crushing some of them to sand and some to fine powder!

Then the winds blew, and they carried cutting tools with them — tiny, sharp-edged grains of hard quartz sand. Whirled by the wind, sand can bore holes in granite cliffs.

At last, great quantities of fire rock had been worn out. Some of it became sand. Some of its ingredients had been powdered to dust as fine as flour. The powdered feldspar formed clay. Fine grains of many minerals formed soft mud.

A rushing flood of water carried the sand and clay and mud down to quieter lakes and oceans. There the particles of ground-up stone dropped to the bottom. Then another flood brought down more particles and dropped them, too. This material deposited by water is called *sediment*. So, layer after layer of sediment settled to the bottoms of the lakes and oceans. At last, the lower layers were buried under a great weight of other layers on top.

Now something began to happen to the lower layers.

glacier

They started to harden. Soft sand and mud and clay turned to stone. The tiny particles became cemented together. Chemicals in the water, helped by the great pressure of the upper layers, did the work.

Scientists have a special name for stones that are made in this way. They call them *sedimentary rocks* because they were made of the materials, called sediment, that the water dropped.

How do the layered rocks climb up out of the lake bottom onto dry land for us to see? Sometimes the water level drops and the rocks are left high and dry. Sometimes an earthquake pushes them up. Sometimes they lift slowly as the rocks underneath push and shove in the earth's crust.

water

mud

hard mud

mud turning to rock

rock

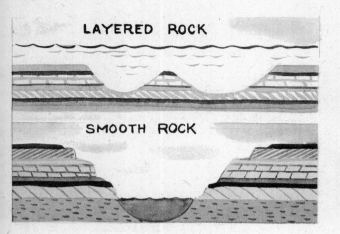

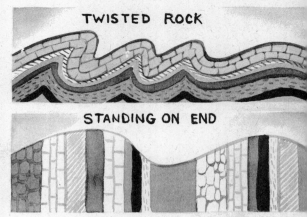

Then new rivers cut gorges in them and you can see the layers almost like pages in a book. They may be bent and twisted, or they may lie smooth and straight as they do in many places in the western part of New York State. Sometimes they may even stand right up on end. In such cases the oldest rocks won't be on the bottom and the newest ones on top. They'll all be standing end-up, side by side.

SANDSTONE

One kind of sedimentary rock is mostly sand grains cemented together. It is called *sandstone*. It is usually made of quartz sand but it may contain other minerals like feldspar (clay) and mica. Sometimes you can see the mica very plainly. You can tell it by its shine.

When you break open a piece of sandstone, it feels rather like a lump of sugar, and sometimes you can see the sand grains. The grains may be as fine as dust or as large as peas.

Grand Canyon

Sandstone comes in many colors, because several minerals were mixed together on the old ocean or lake floor. You may find a pure white specimen or a gray one. Or you may find some that are yellow, brown, red, green or a beautiful pale lavendar.

You will find the most striking colors of all if you make a trip to the Grand Canyon of the Colorado, in Arizona. The high cliffs of the canyon are made of brightly colored bands of sandstone. In the light of sunrise and sunset they make one of the most beautiful pictures in the world. As you look at them, you can see the layers that were piled one on top of another millions of years ago. The colors are due to the iron in the sandstone. It is hard to imagine that these tall canyon walls were once deep under the sea.

sandstone

You need not go to Arizona for a piece of sandstone. In many cities, steps and window sills of houses are made of red sandstone. In other places, the sidewalks are made of a rock called *flagstone*, which is a fine-grained sandstone.

Although sandstone comes in layers, you can often find specimens that are rounded — large chunks and loose pebbles. The picture shows how the wind and weather have smoothed and worn sandstone into odd toadstool shapes.

PUDDING STONE

You have probably noticed that smoothly-rounded pebbles are left lying on the sand along the sides of streams. Long ago this happened, too. When the pebbles and sand were cemented together and turned to hard rock, a curious stone called *conglomerate* or *pudding stone* was made. It's a conglomeration of various things. If the grains in sandstone are larger than a pea, we call it conglomerate. Sometimes the "grains" in the sandstone are as large as boulders.

40

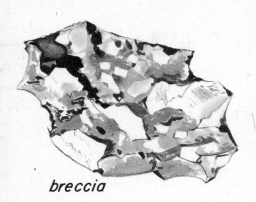
breccia

pudding stone

BRECCIA

A special kind of mixture is formed when broken chips of rock fall into soft mud. When this hardens into stone, it is called *breccia*. The hard chunks in breccia have sharp edges. The edges show that the chunks were never rolled downstream and smoothed off like the pebbles in conglomerate.

SHALE

Sometimes the flood waters of long ago dropped fine-powdered clay or mud on the ocean floor, with little or no sand mixed in it. Then the sedimentary rock that formed was called *shale*.

Shale looks as if it were hardened mud and clay. It is often very soft and crumbly, and in thin layers which are easy to tear apart.

Sandstone that has extra-fine grains is also called shale. This shale is harder and less crumbly than the kinds that come from clay and mud.

41

shale

PICTURE-BOOKS IN STONE

Even if it is fairly hard, shale is easy to split along the layers. Often you can see the marks made by currents of water thousands of years ago, showing that the layers were built by floods. Very often the layers are filled with the remains of little shells and sea animals or marked by the tracks of creatures that walked upon the mud long ago.

The layers of rock are like the pages of a book. Dig out a layered slice and there is a kind of picture in stone of a clam, a coral, a snail, a fish or a frond of fern. These pictures are the prints or outlines of real animals and plants that lived when the rock they are found in was still soft mud. They died and the mud covered them. After the soft parts of the animals were gone, the hard outside skeletons were imprinted in the new-forming rock, making perfect life portraits. These printed pictures are called *fossils*. Fossil comes from a Latin word that means something dug up.

LIMESTONE

While the ancient rivers were carrying down sand and mud from the mountains, something else was happening in the oceans—something that made an entirely different kind of sedimentary rock. This rock we might call *life-rock*, because once-living creatures built it.

The first life on earth was in the sea. Tiny simple sea plants and sea animals were the first living things. After a while, some began to form hard shells. Some of them were so tiny that one or two of them alone could scarcely be seen. Others were as large as snails or clams. Billions and billions of these creatures lived in the oceans. When they died their shells sank to the bottom. Layer after layer of shells piled up on the ocean floor.

All this while, tiny coral animals called *polyps* were also living and dying and leaving their skeletons on the sea bottom. Each one built on top of the other until, finally, whole coral islands rose above the level of the sea.

Shells and corals and some kinds of little sea plants built the life-rock we call *limestone*.

shells

Limestone is very much like the mineral, calcite. Remember how we scratched and tested them? Both are made mostly of a substance called *lime*. Lime is the stuff that fizzes when you test specimens with soda water.

How did lime get into the sea?

The calcite on the land dissolved in rain water, and in the brooks and rivers. The rivers carried it to the sea.

Only shellfish and corals and a few little sea plants are able to take the lime from the water. When they die and pile up on the ocean bottom they build limestones.

Some kinds of limestone formed in places where the shells were mixed with sand or mud or other minerals. These kinds are gray or yellow, red or brown, or almost black.

Some of the finest fossils are found in limestone. Whole pieces of ancient sea bottom are now high and dry on land. In them we find shells, corals, and many other long-dead sea creatures.

lagoon

sea level

barrier island

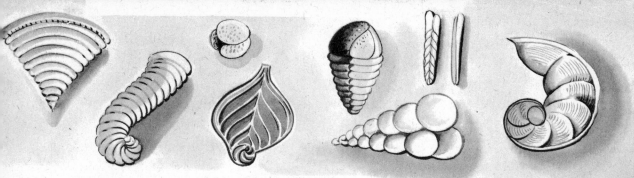

fossilized animals which form chalk

CHALK

An interesting kind of limestone is chalk—real chalk, not the commercial kind you use for writing on blackboards. Chalk is made of the tiny shells of ancient sea animals—shells so tiny you can't see them with your naked eye. Yet millions of them built the beautiful White Cliffs of Dover along the English Channel.

Try the soda water test on a piece of real chalk.

A LIMESTONE THAT'S DIFFERENT

Most limestone was built of shells and corals in the sea, but some limestone comes up out of the earth. Hot springs and geysers bubble or shoot out water full of lime. When the water evaporates it leaves limey deposits. Rock like this, that is found around springs, is called *tufa*.

45

geyser

COAL

Long ago, great steamy jungles and swamps covered parts of the world where the weather now is cool. In Pennsylvania and many other places where the great coal mines are found today, it was just like the tropics. Giant ferns, queer ancient trees and plants grew and died and were buried in the swamps. New ones grew on top of them. Layer after layer of dead plants piled up in the ooze. You can guess what happened. Under great pressure and after millions of years there was another kind of sedimentary rock — a rock built by once-living plants. We call it *coal*.

It's easy to find a bit of fossil fern in common coal. You may even find a leaf of the ginkgo tree, a kind of tree still alive in the world today.

47

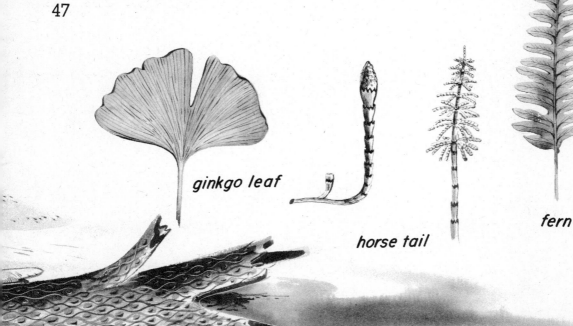

ginkgo leaf

horse tail

fern

Meet the earth

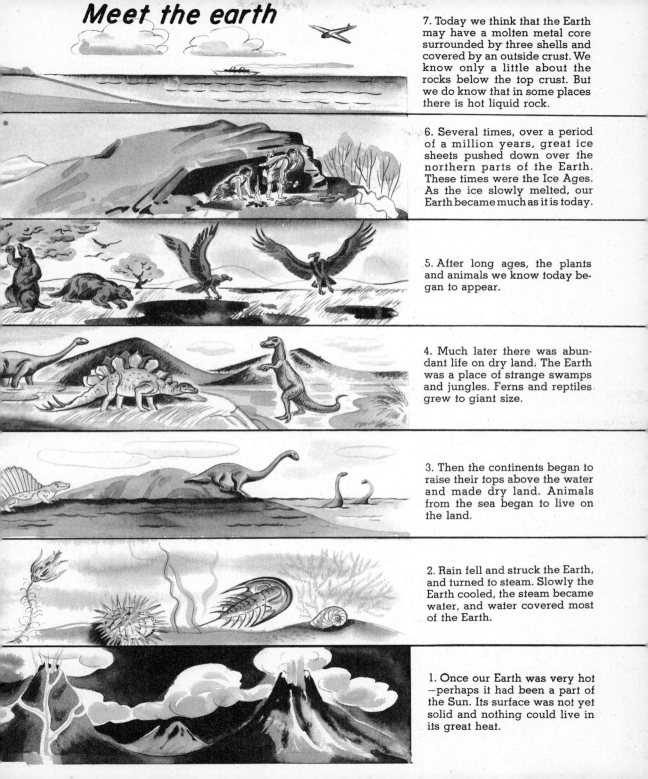

7. Today we think that the Earth may have a molten metal core surrounded by three shells and covered by an outside crust. We know only a little about the rocks below the top crust. But we do know that in some places there is hot liquid rock.

6. Several times, over a period of a million years, great ice sheets pushed down over the northern parts of the Earth. These times were the Ice Ages. As the ice slowly melted, our Earth became much as it is today.

5. After long ages, the plants and animals we know today began to appear.

4. Much later there was abundant life on dry land. The Earth was a place of strange swamps and jungles. Ferns and reptiles grew to giant size.

3. Then the continents began to raise their tops above the water and made dry land. Animals from the sea began to live on the land.

2. Rain fell and struck the Earth, and turned to steam. Slowly the Earth cooled, the steam became water, and water covered most of the Earth.

1. Once our Earth was very hot —perhaps it had been a part of the Sun. Its surface was not yet solid and nothing could live in its great heat.

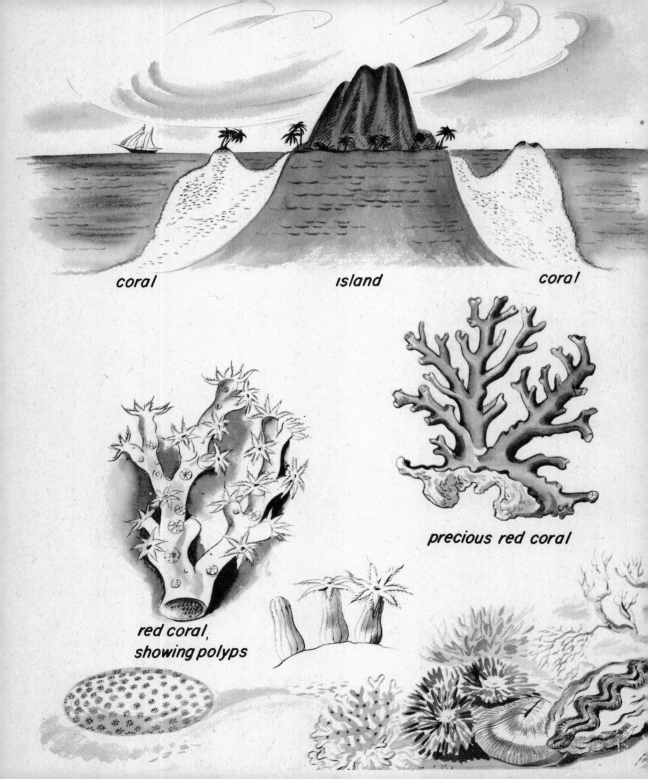

coral   island   coral

precious red coral

red coral,
showing polyps

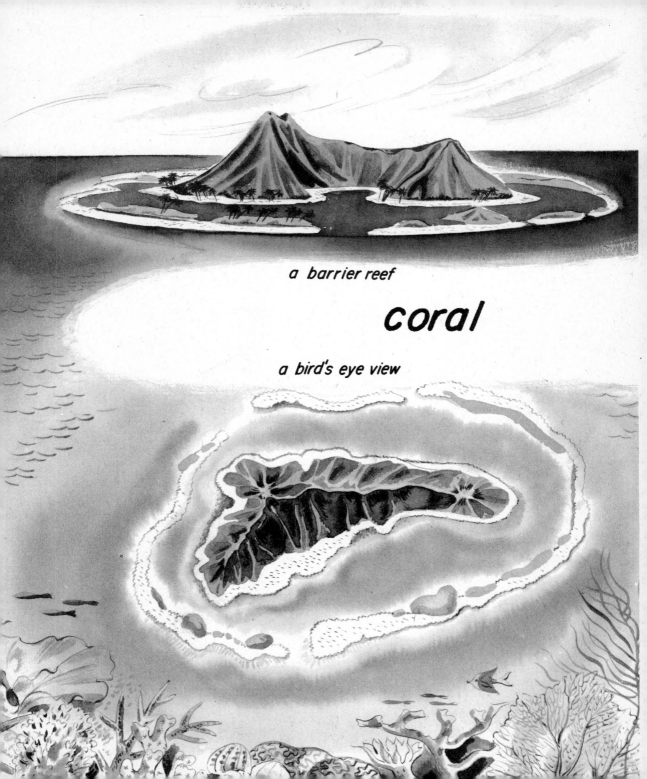

a barrier reef

coral

a bird's eye view

water

wind

Elements at Work on Stone

Carlsbad Cavern,
New Mexico

Weyers Cave,
Virginia

MADE-OVER ROCK

Now you have specimens of igneous or fire rocks, such as granite and lava. You also have sedimentary rocks made in several different ways:

1. Made from broken-up grains of other rocks dropped on the sea bottom
2. Built by the shells and skeletons of animals
3. Made from the remains of ancient plants

There is still another kind of rock. Scientists call it *metamorphic rock*, which means *changed* or *made-over* rock. This is how it was formed:

You remember that the hot, doughy magma can flow underground, pushing other rocks up or away from it. Sometimes magma has squeezed and pressed in such a way that it actually has bent and folded great sections of the earth's surface. Whole layers of surface rock were squeezed by the folding. Pressure, and heat from the fiery magma, changed that surface rock and made it over into a new kind of rock. Sometimes water and chemicals helped in making the change.

Let's see what happens when some of the stones you already know are made over into metamorphic rock.

CROSS SECTION OF A MOUNTAIN RANGE

GNEISS

Granite changes into a stone called *gneiss*, which is pronounced "nice."

Gneiss is not speckled like granite. Instead, it has light and dark streaks like a piece of marble cake. Sometimes the bands are straight, but usually they are twisted and bent. Heat and pressure made the light and dark ingredients of granite separate from each other. The light speckles came together into the light-colored bands and the dark speckles collected in the dark bands. Each mineral has been sorted out into its own layer.

MARBLE

Limestone changes into *marble*.

When you break open a piece of marble it often looks like a lump of sugar. You can see little shiny clear grains in it. Very often you will find wavy twisted bands of color in marble, too. They are the same colors you find in limestone — gray, yellow, pink, red or black.

57

gneiss   *marble*

marble quarry

white marble

You can scratch marble with a copper penny, and it fizzes if you pour soda water over it.

Buildings are often decorated with marble because it can be cut and polished beautifully.

WHEN SANDSTONE CHANGES

Sandstone can be changed by heat and pressure into several different stones.

Remember how sand was made in the beginning, and you will see why. Sometimes sand is mostly ground-up quartz or quartz with feldspar. Sometimes it is ground-up granite, which is a mixture of quartz, feldspar and mica and maybe other minerals, too.

Suppose your sandstone was mostly quartz. Then heat and pressure changed it into a stone called *quartzite*. When you first look at a specimen of quartzite, you may think it is limestone or marble — a freshly-broken piece has a sugary look. But you can make two tests:

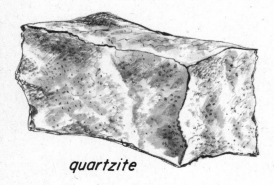
quartzite

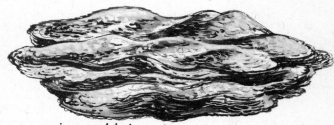
mica schist

1. See how hard the stone is. You can scratch lime-stone or marble with a copper penny, but you cannot scratch quartzite. In fact, you can use your quartzite to scratch a piece of glass!
2. Pour soda water on it. Limestone or marble will fizz a lot, quartzite will not.

But suppose your sandstone was made from sand of a different sort. Suppose it was ground-up rock that had a lot of mica in it. Heat and pressure made this kind of sandstone into *mica schist* (pronounced "shist" to rhyme with mist). It looks like mica all ground up with something else, which is just what it is.

When you break open a piece of mica schist, it has a sparkly look, from the flecks of mica in it. And you can see thin, wavy layers running through it — layers of quartz and mica.

Sometimes mica schist is silvery or light gray. More often it is dark gray or brownish or even black because of other minerals mixed in the sand.

SLATE

Shale changes into *slate*.

Remember that shale is hardened mud or clay. It is usually rather crumbly and soft. Heat and pressure make it over into a hard stone that does not crumble.

Slate can be split easily into thin layers, so it is often used on the roofs of houses. It is so smooth that long ago children did their lessons on thin pieces of slate at school. For slate pencils, they once used the spines of sea urchins, little lime-covered animals that live in the sea. The blackboard in your school today is probably slate. Slate is usually gray or black but it may be brown, red, green or purple.

sea urchins

coal mine

COAL CAN CHANGE, TOO

Soft coal can change into hard coal. Once soft coal itself was fragments of moss and other plants. Some soft coal was made over into hard *anthracite*.

Anthracite under tremendous heat and pressure and just the right conditions turns into a mineral called *graphite*. You can write perfectly well with a chunk of graphite. The "lead" in your lead pencil is mostly graphite.

In Rhode Island, there is a coal mine where the coal is almost turned to graphite. As coal to burn, it is just about the worst in the world. It is so hard to burn they use it to line furnaces! But as a specimen of stone it is very interesting.

ORES

If you live in mining country you probably have picked up specimens that miners call *ores*.

61

An ore is a rock that contains metal. Some metals like gold, silver and copper may occur in whole solid chunks that you can hack out of the rocks. We call these metals *native gold*, *native silver*, *native copper*. Native iron does not occur on earth. It is found only in meteorites, or shooting stars, that drop from the sky.

Most metals do not occur in their pure form. The ores have to be sent to a smelter where the metal is separated from the rock.

Quartz and gold are often found together. Copper may be mixed with many things. Iron is found in many sorts of rocks. Remember how it colored many minerals we have talked about.

THIS ONE IS A MAGNET!

If you live in New York, Pennsylvania or New Jersey, you may find a special kind of black iron ore called *magnetite*. It can pick up needles or bits of iron filings almost as well as a little horseshoe-shaped magnet you buy at the store. They say magnetite got its name from Magnes, a shepherd who lived long ago in Greece,

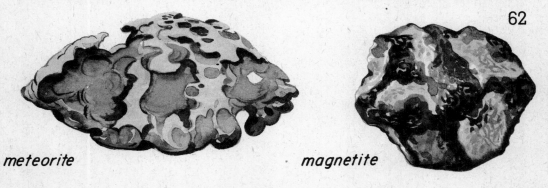

meteorite   *magnetite*

who discovered that this queer black iron ore attracted the tip of his iron-pointed staff.

Compass needles were once just slivers of magnetite. Since these slivers always pointed toward the North Star, called the lode (or leading) star, the mineral got the name *lodestone*. Columbus had a crude compass made of a sliver of lodestone and he carried a spare piece in case his compass needle lost its magnetism on the voyage.

Magnetite isn't like any black rock you've had before. It's heavy when you lift it in your hand — you'd know at once it had metal in it. Stick a pen point on it and see if it holds. It can be found with fire rocks or made-over rocks.

OTHER IRON ORES

A famous kind of iron ore is *iron pyrite*, called *fool's gold*, although this name is better used for *copper*

63

pyrite which is much more golden in color. It *has* fooled people, even miners, who thought they had real gold. It comes in cubes, shiny as brass, but you can make a test to prove what your specimen is. Scratch it across the piece of tile in your testing kit. You will see that it leaves a greenish-black streak. Gold makes a true yellow streak. And gold is soft — not brittle like fool's gold.

If you have a piece of red iron ore it is *hematite*. It leaves a blood-red streak on your tile.

If your ore is yellowish brown to dark brown, it is *limonite*. It gives a yellow-brown streak. Both hematite and limonite are used in making paints.

COPPER ORES

Green copper ore is called *malachite*. Its streak is green.

Blue copper ore is called *azurite*. Its streak is blue.

In some places in the world these ores are so plentiful that they tinge the rivers with deep blue or green. Often the two ores are found together.

You find beautiful malachite in New Mexico and in Russia. The czars had ornaments made from great slabs of it. They even used it for table tops.

malachite

garnet

gypsum

GARNET

Sometimes when you break open a piece of mica schist, you find chunks of red or brown minerals. When you examine them you find that they are smooth-sided crystals that look like cubes with the corners cut off. They have a dull glossy surface. They are *garnets*.

Sometimes garnets may be green. Look for garnets, for they are found in widely-scattered places. You will be most likely to have luck on a garnet hunt if you live in Colorado, New York, New Hampshire or North Carolina.

GYPSUM

Here is a stone that may have fooled you, especially if you live in Texas, Colorado, New Mexico or upper New York. It is white. It is soft — you can scratch it with a penny. But it doesn't fizz like calcite or limestone.

It is a mineral called *gypsum*. Actually, gypsum is softer than calcite. You can scratch it with your finger nail.

GEODES

One of the most interesting specimens to find is a curious thing called a *geode*. This is an irregular-shaped ball of rock that has a hollow inside it. When you break it open, you will find the hollow partly filled with crystals. Often they are quartz, and six-sided; or they may be calcite — perhaps pointed dogtooth spar crystals. A geode is a kind of surprise package — a little treasure box.

TURQUOISE

If you live in the Southwest, you may find specimens of blue or green turquoise. The Indians polished it and used it for jewelry. They set it in silver.

PETRIFIED WOOD

Petrified wood is really a kind of quartz. When it is cut and polished, you can see the rings in it, exactly like rings in a living tree. This is how it was formed:

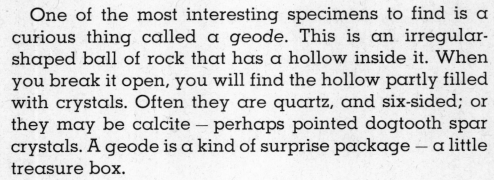

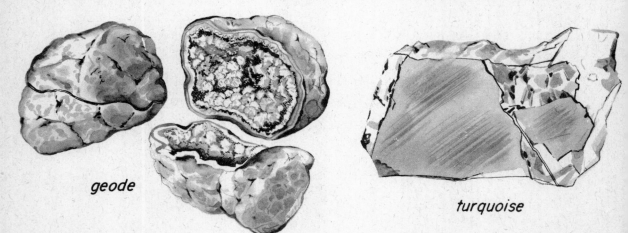

geode

turquoise

Quartz is made of a substance called *silica*. Often silica is dissolved in water. Ancient trees fell into lakes or swamps where there was a great deal of silica dissolved in the water. The water seeped into the tiny cells of which the wood was composed and filled the cells with silica which hardened there. When the fibers of the wood decayed, in their place was hard quartz making a stone picture of the original tree. Now, in places where the swamps dried up, you can find petrified trees lying on dry ground.

So, a petrified tree is not really a tree turned to stone. It is a tree in which stone has taken the place of the original wood. It makes beautiful ornaments and takes a high polish.

SALT

The salt that you eat on your food is really a mineral. Its name is *halite*.

Here is an experiment you can do, and at the same time you can make a genuine halite crystal specimen

67

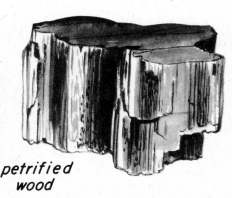

petrified wood

for your collection: Boil a cup of water. Pour into it a few spoonfuls of table salt. When all the salt is dissolved, pour the water into a cup. Now put the cup on a shelf in a cool place where it will not be disturbed for several days. Choose a shelf that has a hook or nail from which you can hang a piece of string so that it falls into the salt water. After three or four days, you will find that salt crystals in perfect little cubes have formed on the string. Take the crystals off carefully and put them in a bottle for your collection. If your mother can spare the space, put the cup and string in the icebox and the crystals will grow faster.

The salt crystals actually grew on the string. Halite crystals grow under the earth — enormous crystals and many of them. They are also called rock salt. Rock salt is mined in many places in the world. Where it comes to the surface, animals use it for a salt lick.

a salt mine

HERE'S WHAT YOU HAVE

Now your collection has these things in it: minerals, rocks, ores.

A *mineral* is made of chemical substances found in nature.

A *rock* is made of a mixture of minerals.

An *ore* is a rock that contains metal.

WHERE TO COLLECT STONES

You can collect stones almost anywhere, even in a big city. When a new building goes up, steam shovels dig rocks out of the earth. If an old building is torn down, you can often find samples of several kinds of stones that were used for walls, window sills, floors or decorations.

69

If you live near a stonecutter's shop, you can pick up chips that come off big blocks of limestone, marble, granite, and other building stones. Some of these specimens may have come from far away. Perhaps the men who work in the shop will tell you about them.

Along the seashore or waterfront you can find sand and pebbles, but sometimes you can also find rocks that have come in ships from far-off countries. When ships have no regular cargo, they often carry a load of stone, called ballast, to keep them from bobbing around on the water. The ballast is dumped overboard when the ship gets a cargo.

Keep your eyes open for places where hills have been cut through to make a level bed for roads or railway tracks. You may find big chunks of interesting rock blasted away.

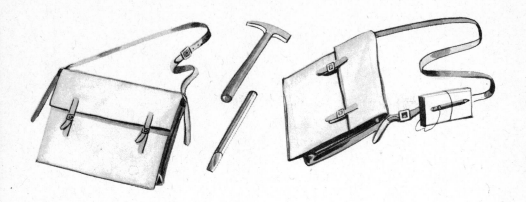

If you live near a mine or a rock quarry, you can find interesting specimens. Some of them may have come up from far beneath the surface of the earth.

Wherever you go, you will be surprised at the many different kinds of stones you can find once you start looking for them.

HOW TO GO ON A REAL COLLECTING TRIP

A real collecting trip is fun. It is most fun of all if you take along the things you need to make it a success.

First, be sure you have your hammer and your chisel.

Next most important is a strong bag in which to carry your specimens. Don't depend on your pockets. They get filled up in no time, then, with both hands full, you are bound to find the finest specimen of all on your way home. The best kind of bag is made of brown canvas and hangs over your shoulder at your side, where you can poke specimens into it easily. (When you start you can carry your tools and lunch in the bag, too.)

Take along pieces of newspaper, cut so that you get four squares out of one big page. You may not want to wrap up every specimen, but you will want to keep some separate from the others. Small crystals wrapped up won't get lost. Wrap up soft stones so that others won't scratch them.

Take with you adhesive tape to label specimens as you find them. Here is a way to make labeling easy: Before you leave home, cut a long strip of adhesive tape into small pieces and stick the separate pieces to a sheet of wax paper. Now take a pen and good ink and number the pieces of tape — 1, 2, 3, 4, and so on. You may find twenty or thirty specimens on a trip. If you don't, you can save the labels and use them on the next trip.

Your outfit is complete except for a notebook and pencil. You can be sure not to lose these if you tie the pencil to the notebook and then tie the notebook by a long string to the strap of your bag.

Most collectors chip or hammer off specimens about the size of your fist, but size doesn't particularly matter. A small stone can be very good. Or you may want an extra-large chunk to show something that is interesting — a wavy band in a piece of gneiss, for example, or the different ingredients in pegmatite, or coarse granite.

As soon as you get a specimen, take one of the numbered pieces of adhesive tape and stick it firmly on the stone. Collectors usually number specimens in the order in which they find them. The first stone they pick up is number 1, the second is number 2.

Next, write the number of the stone in your notebook, and after it tell where you found the stone. Here are some of the ways you can make this kind of entry in your notebook:

1. Wall along Honey Hollow Road, near Katonah, New York
2. Rocks at seashore, Newport, Rhode Island
3. Flagstaff Mountain, Boulder, Colorado
4. Pebble from Laguna Beach, California
5. Iron ore, Jones Mine, Lake Superior, Minnesota

Don't put off writing in your notebook till you get home. You may pick up several rocks that look quite a bit alike. Later, you may not be able to remember where you got which one.

(Later on, you will see why the adhesive tape numbers and the notebook are very good ideas, even though they take a little time.)

Real collectors look at many things besides the stones lying on the ground. Suppose you come to a steep ledge of rock. See if there are different layers showing in the ledge. Take specimens of each layer, and make a note in your book telling which stone came from the top layer and which from the bottom layer. When you begin to identify the stones, you may be able to tell interesting things about how they were

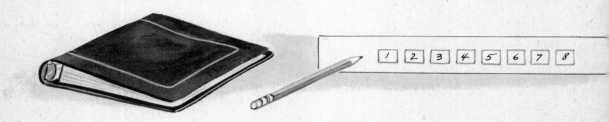

made. Is the bottom layer a sedimentary stone, such as shale? Are the upper layers granite? Then maybe you have seen a place where, long ago, magma pushed its way up and over a layer of sedimentary stone.

It is usually a good idea to bring home two specimens of each stone if you can. One you can put in your collection and the other you can use for testing or trading. Although a stone may not look like anything special when you pick it up, perhaps it is one that other collectors are eager to have and you may be able to trade it for something else you want.

This is the way you keep your duplicates straight: You can bring along two sets of numbered stickers, or you can write the number on a page torn out of your notebook and wrap it up with the duplicate in a sheet of newspaper.

WHAT TO DO WHEN YOU GET HOME

Maybe you wanted to take your testing kit and your book along on your first trip. There is no reason why you shouldn't, except that they are awkward to carry. But, as a rule, it is more fun to bring your stones home first and then see what you have.

Now you can see how useful the adhesive tape stickers and the notebook are.

Suppose you test a specimen and find that it is a piece of marble. It is the fifteenth stone you have collected. Look up number 15 in your notebook. Write *marble* on the same line with the number and the name of the place where you found it.

Next, you can do one of two things: You can make a new adhesive tape label and stick it on the stone like this:

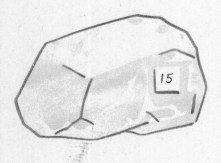

No. 15

MARBLE

Quarry at Westerly R.I.

Or you can use a different system which most collectors follow. They leave the number on the stone. Then they store the specimen in a box or on a shelf. On a card they write out its name and where it was found and thumbtack the card to the shelf in front of the stone.

But suppose you lose the label. Or suppose someone who isn't careful comes to visit. He picks up some specimens and can't remember which boxes they came from. It doesn't matter. You can always look up the number in your notebook. Then you can be sure that number 15 is marble, and you should put the stone back with the label that says *marble*.

HOW TO KEEP A STONE COLLECTION

Here are the easiest ways to keep your collection:

Arrange the stones by number, then store them in little wooden boxes or cut-down shoe boxes or, better still, on open shelves or in empty drawers of an old dresser.

The pictures show what to do with the labels. The important thing is to find containers with sides that are not too high. Sides help keep the stones where they belong. The tops on boxes keep off dust, and they also make it possible to pile boxes up if you need to save space.

77

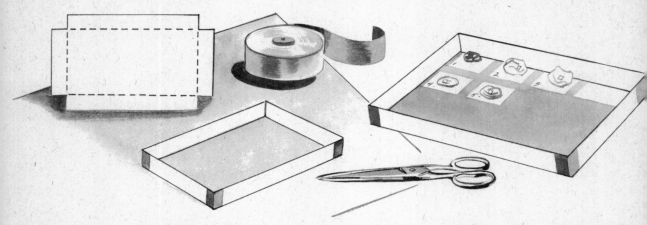

Cardboard egg cartons make fine containers for small specimens but they do get broken easily.

It is a good idea to have a few small clear glass bottles around, too. You can keep samples of sand in them, or small crystals that might easily be lost from boxes. Small cardboard jewelry boxes are very good for lightweight specimens.

Keep a separate box or drawer for your duplicates, and be sure to label them with the same numbers as the specimens in your main collection. You don't need to name each one, because you can always look up the number in your notebook and see what it is.

If you have empty bookshelves, they are best of all because there you can see all your specimens and handle them easily. You do have to dust shelves, but you won't mind too much, if collecting becomes a real hobby.

Try to keep the boxes in some place where you can get at them easily but also where they will not be in the way.

HOW TO MAKE SHELVES FOR A COLLECTION

If you want shelves for your collection, you can make them from wooden grocery-store boxes. Then you can either store your small boxes on the shelves or arrange the stones right on open shelves.

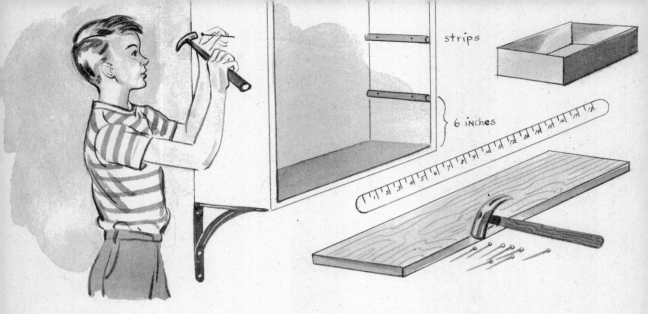

strips

6 inches

First, decide how high the shelves should be. If you want to pile two cigar boxes on top of each other, you should allow about 6 inches between shelves. That is about the right distance, too, if you plan to keep your stones in the open. You need enough space so that you can see the specimens and get at them easily.

With a ruler, measure and mark the places for each shelf on both sides of the box. Be very careful to make the marks at exactly the same height on each side. If you don't, your shelves will slant. Now draw a line from front to back with a small try square or triangle or a ruler: Draw a line on each side for each shelf. Next, nail a thin strip of wood inside the box exactly along each line. These strips are the supports for your shelves.

When you are hammering the thin strips on, be sure to lay the box on its side on a piece of waste wood. Then if the nails go clear through the wall of the box, they won't make holes in the floor or table. Bend the ends of the nails over so that they will not scratch anything, and cover them with small pieces of adhesive tape.

Now make your shelves. They can be pieces from other boxes, or sheets of thin plywood or any other thin wood you can find. Measure before you saw your shelves to make sure they are exactly the right width. After your shelf is cut, slide it on top of the strips you have nailed to the sides of the box.

If you want to make the shelves solid, measure the same distance on the *outside* of the box that you measured on the inside, and draw lines across with your try square or triangle. Now drive small nails through the box, just a little above these outside lines. The nails will hit exactly into the wood of the shelf and keep it firmly in place. You might miss the wood if you didn't have the lines and tried to guess where the nails should go.

You can paint the box shelves if you want to, but the main thing is to have plenty of space for stones without taking up too much room.

Specimen No. 1 Quartz Crystal
Collected at Limerock R. I.
Date March 1 1950
Crystal Shape - six sided
Fracture Shell-like
Color - Clear Colorless
Streak - None
Luster - Glassy
Transparency - Highly
          Transparent
Hardness No. 7

Specific Gravity or Weight
compared to weight of water
                    2.65
Composition - Silica & Oxygen
Formula - SiO_2
Characteristics
    Will scratch glass easily
Varieties - Rock crystal is
    a variety of Quartz
Where found - In Caves
Famous collection places
Alps Brazil Japan
Uses Jewelry, crystal balls

YOUR NOTEBOOK IS IMPORTANT

Remember to keep your notebook in a handy place near your collection. Every time you find out something new about a stone, you can look up its number and write down what you have discovered. This may not seem important at first, but when your collection grows you will not be able to remember everything about each specimen. Later on, you may want to rearrange your collection in new ways, and you will want all your notes to help you keep things straight.

MORE FUN WITH YOUR COLLECTION

As your collection grows you can have fun arranging it in different ways.

You can put together in one section all the rock-making minerals. In another section, put all igneous or fire-made rocks; in another, all sedimentary or layered rocks; in another, all metamorphic or changed (made-over) rocks.

Or you can put together in one section all the stones that come from your own neighborhood and, in another section, all stones from farther away.

You can arrange part of your collection to show good examples of cleavage — the ways stones break — or of especially beautiful colors, or of a number of interesting crystal shapes.

MINERALS   IGNEOUS ROCKS   SEDIMENTARY ROCKS   METAMORPHIC ROCKS

fossil fern

As you find out more about sedimentary rocks, you can arrange them according to their age! There really are ways to tell how old a sedimentary rock is. And it's easy! Fossils of very simple plants and animals are found in the oldest rocks. Fronds or leaves of much higher plants and remains of different animals appear in the newer rocks.

When you rearrange your collection, be sure that the original number is still stuck on each specimen so that you won't get it mixed up with others that may look like it.

All this changing-around will be perfectly safe if you have your notebook handy. If labels get mixed up, you can always check with your book and find out where they belong.

HOW TO JOIN A ROCK CLUB

Most science museums have a Rock and Mineral Club. Ask if you may join. Then you will be taken on field trips to good collecting places near your home.

HOW TO TRADE ROCKS AND INCREASE YOUR COLLECTION

Ask your rock club members about trading specimens.

Consult the magazine, *Rocks and Minerals* (the address is given later). It will give you addresses of collectors who wish to trade.

WHERE YOU CAN FIND OUT MORE ABOUT ROCKS

If you live in a city where there is a science museum, you can find out a great deal about stones by studying the museum's collection.

You can subscribe to a magazine which comes out every two months. It is called *Rocks and Minerals* and it costs $3.00 a year. The address is Peekskill, N. Y.

The American Museum of Natural History, 78th Street and Central Park West, New York, N. Y. has four beautifully-illustrated little books about rocks which they will send you if you mail them 50 cents for each book. The titles are *Stories Read from the Rocks*, *The Earth's Changing Surface*, *The Earth, a Great Storehouse* and *America's Minerals*.

The stones you have read about in this book are only a very few of the many, many kinds in the world. When you get to be a more expert collector, you will want to find out about more of them. You will also want to make chemical tests that will tell what your specimens are. A book called *Minerals* by Herbert S. Zim and Elizabeth K. Cooper, published by Harcourt, Brace and Company, gives directions for many chemical tests that can be made with inexpensive materials. It also tells a great deal about important minerals.

The Rock Book by C. L. and M. A. Fenton, published by Doubleday & Company, Inc., might be a little hard for you to read, but it has wonderful pictures in it and it will be useful if you have an older person to help explain it.

And the most useful book of all is *Field Book of Common Rocks and Minerals* by F. B. Loomis, published by G. P. Putnam's Sons. It has just about everything you need to know.

DO YOU KNOW THAT:

Amber is a beautiful yellow mineral that was once the resin of ancient pines and became a fossil when the trees were buried. Sometimes you can see insects in it that were caught there centuries ago.

There is a mineral called asbestos that comes in long silky fibers that can be picked apart like thread. It will not burn or melt.

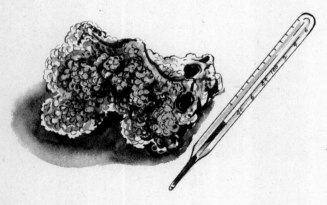

Cinnabar is a bright red mineral that is found around hot springs. Mercury comes from it and is used in thermometers and barometers.

Pitchblende is a black mineral from which radium comes. It is scarce and very important to scientists. Sometimes you can see radium shining in pitchblende.

asphalt lake in Hancock Park, Los Angeles

In some places oil has oozed up through the ground and changed into lakes of asphalt or pitch. It is used for roads and roofing. There are asphalt lakes in California and Trinidad.

The American Indians mined copper. They dug it from the Upper Peninsula in Michigan to use for knives, awls and ornaments.

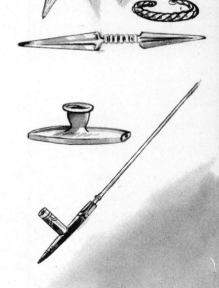

In southwest Minnesota, near Pipestone, are the quarries where the Indians used to cut the red stone for their peace pipes.

The tin mines in Cornwall, England, are among the world's oldest. The ancient Romans knew about them, and the Phoenician traders sold the tin to Mediterranean people to mix with copper to make bronze.

Beautiful and Useful Things Made of Stone

INDEX

pebble porphyry

red coral

garnet

flint arrowhead

quartz crystal

malachite

magnetite

dogtooth spar

quartzite

obsidian

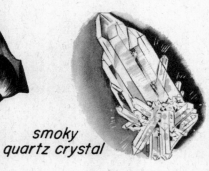

smoky
quartz crystal

porphyry